Intermediate Guide to Pattern Fitting and Alteration

Table of Contents

Introduction

On one level, finding any piece of cloth to cover the body might be said to be easy. But putting together clothing that properly identifies, presents, and makes an individual feel comfortable and proud requires some creativity and professionalism. The art of modern pattern fitting and alteration aims to make something outstandingly unique out of a simple already-made cloth or a plain fabric.

There are so many reasons why clothing is important. It might be for modesty, comfort, presentation, or plain survival. The kind of clothes you put on your body would, firstly, be judged by how they fit you. Anybody can try on any clothing, but they most likely won't try on something that doesn't fit.

Most of the time, our preferences for what fits our bodies are affected by what we feel most comfortable in. This is where individualism comes in. Every cloth or pattern will not be suitable for everyone. In most cases, eight out of ten persons would require a unique fitting for their clothing. You would have to consider the shape of the individual. Commercial pattern makers work with pre-existing models and structures, but we all know very few of us meet those standards. As such, drafting the right pattern for the right fit for an individual means that you have to consider every curve and mold on the individual's body, and the usual idea is to flatter the right places. Being able to alter patterns and create new fittings also makes individuals feel unique in their own right.

This is the art and the essence of the sewing industry. Basically, if you can't get the patterns to fit, then, most likely, your finished product will not come out right. Those who have started out in fashion have to see that making patterns is one of the most challenging parts of sewing, but a good pattern maker makes a great designer, hence a great sewer. There are those who have started down this road, and then they feel like this path might be too cumbersome for them. You might not want to go through all the mathematics and measurements involved in creating your precise fitting. Then it is not too late for you to change course. The devil is in the details. You would have to go through the steps outlined in this book and create what is needed for you to become a great pattern fitter and alteration expert. In this guide, you'll notice that we place more emphasis on patterns to enhance your designer approach.

A career is not built in a day; it is built over time based on your works and your reputation in the industry. The goal of this guide is to equip you with what it takes to create a pattern that fits with the mind of a designer. The bottom line is making something better out of whatever fabric or simple dress is in your hand. Also, don't forget that beauty is in the eyes of the beholder. Your intention should always be to make something that looks better on a person wearing the clothing, something that is properly fitted and which accentuates their body.

Of course, there are commercial patterns available for general clothing, but you may want to create unique pieces for designs and improve on already-made clothes. Perhaps you want to make something bolder out of already existing designs. If so, this guide is for you.

If you haven't already done so, I would ask you to read my companion book, the beginner's guide to pattern fitting. You'll see in that the basics of pattern-drafting and sewing constructions.

In this intermediate guide, we'll be diving deeper into a semi-advanced level of pattern making, fitting, and alteration. I'll show you examples of how you can get creative with making patterns and alterations. We will touch on some beginner's points as a reminder, but will mainly focus on advanced-level methods to show you ways of how to create patterns with expertise and creativity. You will learn how to manipulate patterns into the perfect fit and draw up your own designs in the process.

This guide covers all the requirements, the use and application of tools and equipment necessary for pattern fitting and alterations. There are many cases where the inability to use the right tools and methods to effect an alteration has been the reason why the end result has gone wrong. Without the right tools in your tool kit, and the knowledge to use them, the results will almost certainly be mediocre. This book will also help you understand the different types and methods of pattern-making and alterations.

We will also be looking into a step-by-step process of how to redesign some simple garments. This will give you hands-on knowledge about how to creatively make your pattern designs.

We will look at how to;

- ❖ Redesign a man's long shirt into a woman's beautiful dress.

- ❖ How to combine two different colored tee-shirts into one.

- ❖ Alter your low waist jeans into a high waist.

- ❖ Make a simple pattern of male trousers.

- ❖ Create a blazer pattern.

- ❖ Create a lady's blouse pattern and experiment with sleeves.

- ❖ Create collars.

At the end of the guide, you should be able to use the step-by-step processes to alter patterns and make new fittings without changing the structure of the clothing.

- → You will know the right tools to use to create perfect patterns and alterations.

→ You should be able to know the different pattern types and pattern methods. You will also be able to know the best ways to apply the pattern methods and what kind of designs are best produced with the different pattern methods that are available.

→ You should be able to create pattern fittings without damaging material or changing the overall measurements of the clothing.

→ You should be able to make professional alterations, understanding the different methods of alterations to create perfect fits. You will be able to use the right alteration method to ensure you produce the perfect piece at the end of the day.

→ You should be able to create your unique designs through alterations and pattern fitting.

Chapter One:
Tools, Equipment, and Accessories

The best pattern creations are made with the right tools and equipment. Not having the necessary sewing tools is like not having the necessary ingredients needed to prepare a meal. Without the right ingredients, that meal won't come out the way the menu described, and it definitely won't taste how it should! No designer would want that result for their proposed idea.

Why are the right tools for pattern fitting and alteration?

1. **Fabric texture/characteristic**: Fabrics are sensitive materials that are factored around precision. Fabrics are designed and made with different textures, designs, and aesthetics. Some fabrics are soft, while others can be hard, stony, or even very light in weight. Using a tool made for a hard fabric on a soft fabric can cause irreparable damage. This could mean more cost for you and time wasted.

2. **Design implementation**: There are some patterns that can only be made when you have specific tools. For instance, to start with block pattern making, you have to get your cardboard or papers handy. If you don't start this correctly, you can make errors, therefore

causing damage. You end up losing your fabric and your time.

3. **Alteration precision**: The best alteration methods can only be carried out with the right tools. Failure to use the right tools can cause damage to your fabric, and, rather than making an alteration, you would end up disfiguring your clothing. For example, tools like seam rippers help quickly loosen the seams and not expand the thread holes.

4. **Effectiveness**: Using the best tools and the right tools ensure that you save time, avoid damage, and consequently save money. For instance, pressing tools can help straighten fabric properly to avoid squeeze, hence helping you make better patterns quickly. Imagine you are the only pattern maker in your design outfit, and you needed to churn out a considerable number before the end of the day. Or, you have a forthcoming event that you must make a dress for. In cases like this, the last thing you would need is a scanty tool bag. The right tool will help you make the most of your time and ensure that you have the kind of quality that you want to put out there.

5. **Durability**: Your tools will last longer when you have all the right tools present at your work table. You might wonder how. This simply means that you won't have to use the wrong scissors or needles for the wrong fabric. Using the wrong ones might mean that you would most likely damage your tool and still be unable to get your desired result. You would be

incurring more costs than you thought you were saving.

6. **Safety**: The importance of a safe working environment cannot be overemphasized. Imagine walking into your sewing store, only to be pierced by a needle in your foot. That could mean no work for you on that day, to say nothing of the pain and inconvenience. Only the right tools and equipment can help ensure that you avoid occupational hazards.

Your work table should have the following categories of tools;

→ Cutting Tools

→ Marking Tools

→ Measurement Tools

→ Pressing Tools

→ Needles

→ Sewing Equipment and Accessories

Cutting tools

Cutting tools are, obviously, a very important part of your pattern making. The kind of cutting tool you use will determine how clean your cut will be. It also affects how fast and smooth you will be able to cut. You can make straight cuts, curve cuts, and angular cuts with these implements.

- **Angled fabric scissors**: They help you make cuts in long and single strokes. Especially when cutting heavy fabrics. They increase your effectiveness.

- **Micro Serrated scissors**: These scissors are great for lightweight materials, especially if you will be working with satins and crepes. They have micro-serrations on the blades to help you hold material firmly to avoid slipping.

- **Paper cutting scissors**: Paper cutting scissors helps you make your pattern on cardboard or paper. This helps keep your fabric scissors as sharp as it should be.

- **Small sharp fabric scissors**: This cutting tool is great for cutting and trimming seam allowances. You can also use it for cutting small motifs for appliques.

- **Duckbill Scissors**: These scissors are specially used with your applique needlework. They help you clip out extra fabric from your work. The paddle-shaped blade helps you cut clearly around your applique stitches. They easily pick at the threads between your work.

- **Pinking shears**: Pinking shears have a zigzag edge that makes them easy for you when finishing your fabric edges. This prevents your edges from fraying and unraveling.

- **Bent scissor**: The bent scissors are designed to have a bent lower blade; this helps keep the blades parallel to the table to help you cut your fabric with more precision.

- **Spring-action scissors**: Spring-action, as the name implies, are scissors that are fortified with a spring; hence, it makes it easier for you to open the blades and cut. This way, you are faster, and you also have less stress on your fingers and wrist. They're great for sewers that might have arthritic or related conditions.

- **Double curved embroidery scissors**: These scissors fit perfectly in embroidery hoops. The blades can easily get into the hoops and tight spaces, making it easy to make cuts during embroidery.

- **Thread Snips**: This tool helps with cutting threads when doing embroidery. It helps you cut out threads easily while sewing. You can get the one that gives you a rope to hang around your neck.

- **Rotary cutters**: Rotary cutters are very effective for cutting heavy materials or more than one material in layers at the same time. If you work with many materials at once, then the rotary cutter will be a very important cutting tool for your work kit. Thick fabrics like faux, felt, vinyl are best to use it with.

- **Buttonhole cutters**: As the name indicates, this tool gives you clean button cuts. Gone are the days where you have to use your scissors to make holes that might be too big or cause damage. Use a buttonhole cutter to make a hole by placing the chisel in the center of the buttonhole and push it down sharply between the thread.

- **Seam rippers**: A seam ripper is a must-have tool, at least if you get on your tailoring table a lot. You can cut open threads easily without damaging the fabric. They help rip the seams off without causing any damage. This is a must-have tool if you're making alterations.

- **Exacto knife**: This helps you make smaller holes in fabrics.

- **Awl:** This tool is useful for feeding gathered fabric into the needle.

Measuring Tools

When it comes to pattern-fitting and alterations, we could say that if 'measurement' is king, then 'cuts' might well be the queen. Using measuring tools helps you transfer the right measurements and make the right adjustments where necessary. Without great measuring tools, you'll be spending a lot of time going back and forth on your work because of significant changes that you might have to make.

- **Measuring tape**: Measuring tape is a must when it comes to tools for sewing. The measuring tape helps you take body measurements, and you can also bend, curve, and wrap the tape to take the kind of measurement you want. It's then easy to transfer this to your cutting paper.

- **L-scale**: Also called the tri-scale. It is mostly made of wood or steel. It is mostly used to draw perpendicular lines or drafting on brown paper. It helps to draw accurate lines. Mostly 90-degree angles and straight edges, it measures, rules, and squares jointly.

- **French curve**: Drawing and cutting smoothly is one of the arts of professionalism, and your French curve ensures you get it right. When it's time to blend in the lines or draw a perfecting smooth curve, then you can lean on the French curve.

- **Clear Ruler**: A clear ruler will help you draft patterns and add your seam allowances.

- **Meter ruler/yardstick**: You can use this to draw lines and create hemlines. You can use this to check for grain lines. It can be metal or wood.

- **Hemline gauge**: A hemline gauge is very useful for your sewing project. It helps you create hems by folding the hem of the fabric as deep as you want it to go. It is made of metal that does not rust. It has markings to measure the space or length of the hem.

- **Buttonhole gauge**: A button guide helps you discover the size of a button to make better holes.

- **Flexible curve**: This is a curvy plastic rule. It is a terrific tool as it can bend to fit whatever shape you want. You can draw curved or straight lines with this. It can be adjusted to fit lines to draw your patterns. Whether straight, curves, or arcs, this is one tool that makes your work really easy.

- **Grading ruler**: These rulers are used to grade patterns by placing the rulers around line curves.

- **Folding ruler**: These are used for pattern measurements and are best when you have a small tool kit. That's because they're foldable and easily stored.

- **Seam gauge**: A seam gauge is used for measuring button placement, hems, waistbands, and more. This is a useful tool in sewing. If you have been sewing for a while, you will know how handy a seam gauge can be.

- **Metric conversion charts**: This tool helps you convert body measures from imperial conversions to metric conversions and vice versa.

Marking tools

Marking tools helps you easily make notes of alterations on your fabric and take note of points you want to come back to. They help you make lines for cutting and sewing.

- **Tailor's chalk**: This is used for marking your fabric. You can transfer lines, mark pattern lines, make lines for darts and cuts. Tailor's chalk comes in different colors. It's intended to rub off the material. However, some materials with special kinds of colors might not be suitable for using tailor's chalk.

- **Disappearing pens**: These pens are also used to make your marks on fabrics for cuts. You can find them in some craft stores. They are designed so that the ink will evaporate after a certain period of time.

- **Tailor's tack**: This is one of the oldest ways of making markings. But it is most effectively used for marking your darts.

- **Tracing wheel**: This tool has multiple teeth; the teeth can either be seated or smooth. It can be used to make slotted perforations. It's also used to transfer markings onto fabric from fabric. You can use tracing paper with this tool or not. Markings that might be best transferred with a tracing wheel include darts, pleats, buttonholes, notches, and placement lines for applique or pockets.

- **Carbon paper**: Carbon papers are essential in pattern-making to prepare patterns and keep them for later use. It helps you make alterations to your pattern without ruining it or causing any damage.

- **Soap**: Soap is used to mark out patterns in sewing and pattern making.

Pressing Tools

Pressing tools help smoothen fabrics to enable better cutting precisions. Some tools are fabric-specific, while others are more effective for smaller areas. The following are pressing tools.

- **Steam Iron**: An iron is very important because it helps flatten out every bump or ridge.

- **Pressing Cloth**: A pressing cloth helps you form a bridge between your pressing iron and your fabric. It is normally a cotton cloth that is placed on the fabric. The iron plate then goes on top of that.

- **Ironing board**: An ironing board is vital for the pressing process.

- **Clapper and the point presser**: This is a tool used to flatten edges, especially for seams, pleats, and darts.

- **Seam roll**: A seam roll is an essential tool used for pressing out curvy edges. It works well in pressing out seams, darts, and zippers.

- **Tailor's Ham**: The tailor's ham is an effective and handy tool used for pattern-making when pressing and molding seams, sleeves, caps, and darts.

- **Sleeve Board**: This helps you increase your precision in pattern-making. It is a small board used for ironing that helps you iron the sleeves all around the edges without having to crease or spoil them. It helps you save space and does a better job of pressing your sleeves.

Sewing Equipment

Your sewing equipment ranges from your sewing machines to items that help you manage and maintain your sewing tools.

Sewing equipment includes;

- **Pincushion**: A pincushion will help you keep your pins in one place, so you can easily pick them up when you need them and replace them when you are done.

- **Bobbins**: Bobbins hold the thread installed below the needle in the sewing machine; they produce thread for the bottom part of your stitch.

- **Presser feet**: This is a useful piece of equipment. It is used to install zippers or insert piping or beaded trim. It holds one side of the material on one side of the needle to enable you to sew.

- **Duster**: Dusters are used to clean crevices in your machine. One will normally come with your sewing machine.

- **Thimble**: This little bucket-shaped tool helps you push needles into your fabric without having to hurt your finger. This way, you can be fast and precise.

- **Screwdriver**: A screwdriver is very handy for when you might need to dismantle a part of your machine that requires cleaning or repair.

Sewing needles

Sewing needles come in different types and sizes. There are hand sewing needles and machine sewing needles. The kind of fabric and type of thread are some of the things that affect the needle that you'd use for your project. Weightier fabrics will require larger sizes of needles and vice-versa.

- **Ballpoint Needles**: A ballpoint needle works well with knits and will slip within the fibers rather than piercing through them.

- **Stretch needles**: Stretch needles are designed to sew elastic clothes like spandex, synthetics, suede, and swimsuits.

- **Denim/jeans needles**: These needles are made for the heavy and thick stuff. They are reinforced to go through these thick layers of fabrics, and you won't have to bother about your needle coming out in one piece.

- **Leather Needles**: These needles are better used for leathers as they have chiseled points to cut through tough substances.

It's always best to use the specific needles for the proposed fabric type to avoid damaging your fabric and spending time replacing needles because of breakages.

Other accessories include:

- **Erasers**: Erasers should be kept together with your pencils to make corrections where necessary on your cardboard and paper.

- **Pencils**: Pencils always come in handy. You'll need them to draw your design sketches on your notepad and make drawings on your cardboard or paper where necessary. They're useful for taking down measurements and notes if you are one of those that prefer writing with a pencil.

- **Table**: Getting a flat surface for your sewing can help you make better patterns and take away a lot of distractions that come with clutter around you. To focus and do better work, you will need a table where you can put your cardboard or fabric down.

- **Glue**: Glues are terrific, especially when making patterns from cardboard and papers.

- **Tissue paper**: Tissue papers are an essential accessory in your tool kit. You can easily use them to wipe away dirt when needed. They always come in handy.

- **Cardboard notepad**: Having a notepad is essential to record all your measurements and keep them in one place. Measurements are the maps of your patterns and design. If you don't have them, you're like a traveler losing the direction of their course.

Maintaining your Sewing Tools and Equipment

1. You should oil your sewing equipment to prevent rust.

2. Keep your tools in their cases or packs if they are not in use. If you do your sewing at home, keeping your tools safe also means safeguarding them from young children, and, in some cases, adults. If your home is like mine, then I can tell that there will be those people who want to breeze into your workspace to use your fabric scissors to cut a piece of paper or their hair. Your equipment is your livelihood, so make sure it's not accessible to other people.

3. Wipe your blades and other equipment clean with a damp cloth when they are dusty or dirty.

4. You can use sewing machine oil to do your oiling. Oiling your blades is a great way to keep the hinges working fine for a long time.

5. You can also sharpen the blades for maintenance when you feel like they are dull.

Chapter Summary

- Using the right tool is essential for creating amazing designs.

- In this chapter, we've provided you with a list of must-have tools you need to make your patterns.

- Learn to care for your sewing tools using these simple tips.

In the next chapter, we will dive into how to identify and make different types of patterns.

Chapter Two:
Methods of Pattern Fitting and Alteration

This chapter will be divided into two subjects, and we're going to discuss Pattern-fitting and Alteration. Pattern-making depends on various factors like gender, age, and regionality. Suitable measurements and study of basic garment patterns are of great help in creating novel designs. There are basic garment pattern garments which have been commercialized over time.

What is Pattern Making?

Pattern-making is the building block of your design. It forms the framework of what you have to sew. It's like the bridge between your idea of a design and what will be eventually constructed. Pattern making starts with drafting the pattern. Patterns can be drafted on any kind of material. However, cardboards are first used for ease of use and other benefits.

When starting a project or, for instance, when cooking, you would need to have an image of the kind of food you want to cook. Let's say you want to prepare pasta. You know how your pasta looks and tastes on a plate. You plan to make it look that way. Next, you would have to list the ingredients you need to purchase to make your pasta. After which, you purchase the ingredients and clean them to make them ready for cooking. Making your pattern is pretty much getting your ingredients ready for your cooking.

Pattern making is laying down the template of the idea or design that you have first drawn out on paper. This is dependent on the kind of design you have put down. Just as the ingredients will be dependent on the kind of food you are making.

Importance of Pattern Making

Why all the fuss about pattern-making? The arts of sewing and fashion design have evolved over the years. But something that remains very crucial to sewing is the fundamental step of pattern-making and fitting. Before we delve into the types and methods of pattern-making, here are some basic important points.

- **Achieving the right fit:** As we have established so far, the crux of every made dress is the fitting. Hence, the importance of fitting cannot be overemphasized. This is the first important reason why we create patterns. It's because you have to achieve fit. If it doesn't fit, you would have to make it fit.

That is why creating patterns is so important. They help you achieve fitting. The body has different molds and curves, and the idea of designing clothing is to come with your unique design that should fit into those molds and curves. To do this, you would have to create something that aligns. Your design and the body form must match. This is where pattern-making comes in. A comprehensive fashion designer should also, ideally, be a great pattern maker.

- **Reducing Error**: Imagine cutting through an expensive silk fabric after taking some measurements, only to find that you have made the cut some inches too small and you haven't made the right curves at the arm areas. There is no going back on this. You can try to correct your errors, which will very likely only lead to more errors, or take out another expensive silk fabric to begin again. There will be neither the time nor the funds to cover your wastage. Pattern helps to reduce errors and save a massive amount of time. This is further understood when you see that you can easily replicate what you have already done on another fabric.

- **Duplicating style:** Pattern making helps you duplicate style for mass production. It can also help you add to a style by carrying out alterations without redesigning from scratch. The whole process is a wonderful way to save time and money while creating perfectly fitted clothing for individuals.

Different Types of Pattern Making

There are different types of patterns. A sloper pattern or a block pattern is a pattern that is already made. These patterns are available for purchase for home or commercial use. Most people that prefer more individually creative designs for a person or style might not find using a sloper or a block pattern is the best option. But, when learning, it is best to use these patterns as they form the fundamentals of your design knowledge. And they help you understand the aesthetics of your pattern-making. Hence, you see the faults and possibly where you can add or improve upon.

The block or slope pattern is developed for everyday wares or clothes that are standardized. Bespoke designers and fashion houses would rather design their own patterns from scratch for their customers.

You may have a dream of starting your own commercial fashion line; maybe you want to open a line of female blouses or men's shirts. Where there might be already available commercial patterns for these, it is unethical to use these commercial patterns if you are going to start your own fashion line. It is something like an unwritten law.

Most of the time, fashion houses will normally hire their own pattern-maker to create patterns for them. Most outfits have at least one pattern-maker employed just to design patterns. The goal of understanding and using the pattern types is to help you understand the fundamentals.

Factors Affecting Pattern-Making

The factors that affect pattern-making generally influence why we choose the kind of clothes we wear. This is important for a designer to take note of because it will determine the type of pattern to use and the method of pattern-making to apply. Let start with:

Age: There are size differences that come with age, especially when you are talking about large variations like adults and infants. The age of an individual, or a group of persons that you might be designing for, can largely affect the pattern. Infants, for instance, might not do well with a sharp dart or an elaborate design. The elderly might not do well with a standard waist-size or waist-cut. This must be considered when making your pattern.

Climate: Climate also affects pattern-making; not only will you have to consider the kind of material that will be used to sew your design, but you'll also have to consider if a pad might be used in certain areas of your production. You might need to allow for more or less seam space.

Figure: The figure of an individual also has a large role to play. For pattern-making methods that restrict the size of the individual the cloth is being made for, you should strongly consider the size of the individual before starting out on your pattern.

Methods of Pattern Making

There are different methods of making patterns: the flat-pattern method, as you might guess, involves the pattern being drawn up on a flat surface. This is the most commonly used method. Other methods like Flat Pattern making, Pinned pattern method, Trial Garment Methods, and Measurement method are also sometimes employed.

Flat Pattern Method

The flat pattern method is the making of patterns on a flat surface, just as the name implies. It involves drafting out your patterns with the measurements you have taken on cardboard or papers.

Measurement tools like rulers and curves are used here. It will also involve the use of tools like the awl, drill, and notcher. The flat pattern method is mostly used to create block or sloper patterns for simple garments. This method is usually made out of paper or cardboard, and does not need to allow for seam allowances. It is mostly used to make basic apparel, especially men's outfits. To become a very skilled pattern-maker, you will have to get proficient with the flat method. It's an excellent way to acquire the fundamental skills. It really is the basis of pattern-making. With this method, you can easily manipulate and alter your design. It is easier to increase size or add to design.

Basic Tools Required

- Flat Surface/Table of standard height

- L-scale

- French Curve

- Ruler

- Pencil

- Measuring tape

Pros of the Flat Pattern Method

- It makes altering patterns easier from your already cut-out basic pattern.

- Commercialization is easier with this method because you can grade your patterns to different sizes with the same basic pattern.

- You can easily redesign an old pattern.

- Most people going to mass production of clothes will normally use flat pattern due to its ease of grading.

Cons of Flat Pattern Method

- The flat pattern method requires professional training because of its standardized basics. You will need to have perfected the art to be a flat pattern-maker.

- Flat pattern method is a 2-dimensional approach; as such, it does not give you a full picture of what your design looks like. It is difficult to imagine the complete nature of your outcome until you get there. Therefore, it is not recommended for complicated designs.

- To make a basic sloper pattern, you will require a full knowledge of pattern and pattern-making.

Pinned-Pattern Method

The pinned-patterned method involves draping a muslin mock-up pattern directly on the form. This is also called Draping. It is a more advanced 3-dimensional form of pattern-making. In this method, you would need an appropriately-sized model to be a form for your pattern-making.

Muslin is a lightweight cotton cloth. This is draped on the form and then pinned on the required areas for your pattern. You can reuse muslin for more than one pattern. Also, this method helps you get a full picture in advance.

Pinned-patterns are mostly used to construct more complicated forms of design, but using a pinned pattern would still take you back to working with your dotted-paper. At the end of the day, before you can work with a drape for a pinned pattern, you would still need to know the basics of flat pattern.

How to drape (The Pinned-pattern Method)

Draping is simply placing a muslin material over your form. Set out all the tools and materials you need, and follow the next steps to create a pattern using the pinned-pattern method.

What you need:

- Muslin

- Disappearing pen/pencil

- Scissors

- Pattern-cutter

- Glue

- Pins

- Dotted paper

- A form

- Tracing Wheel

- Hip curve

- French Curve

- Tape Measure

- ❏ **Step 1- Set aside your form/model**: The form you set aside should represent the kind of pattern you would be making. For instance, if you're making a pattern for a women's skirt or a basic bodice, you should have a whole form for both patterns. If you have a form that starts from the waist for the women's skirt, or you have a form that ends at the waist for a basic back bodice, you should also have forms that will reproduce this. In this guide, I will be taking you through the steps of making a pattern for a basic bodice.

❏ **Step 2- Place your Muslin on the model**: Take a piece of the muslin material and place it at the back of the form. Spread it out, starting from the neck down to below the waist area, then use a pin to firmly hold the muslin to the model at the lower part of the neck. The pin should not be pushed straight into the model; it should be pushed toward the right side of the model to firmly hold your muslin in place. Continue to place the pins in the areas you want your material to cover. You can cut out the end parts of the material that are obviously not in use on the area. Use your pen to mark out the arm area, the neck, and the dart line.

❏ **Step 3- Cut out the extra material**: Cut out all the extra materials that are not part of the marked areas. Take out your marked muslin. This material is now used to make a pattern using your dotted paper.

❑ **Step 4- Trace your pattern:** Place your dotted paper on the flat table and place your muslin on the paper. Pick up your tracing wheel and run it on the marked lines on your muslin. You can run it over again, maybe twice or thrice, to be sure that it has been properly traced on your dotted paper.

❑ **Step 5- "True" Your Pattern**: Now that the pattern is traced on the dotted paper. You will have to "true it." Truing your tracing is simply making your tracing bolder and better. Take off your muslin on the dotted paper. This is where your French curve and your clear ruler are useful. Use them and a pencil to draw on your tracing. Use the French curve for the arm area and other curved areas.

Your pattern is ready for use.

Considerations when draping

- Remember to retrace using your tracing wheel until visible traces are noticed.

- Use a pattern cutter for a smoother cutting process.

- Use a disappearing pen or chalk that you can wipe off from your muslin, just in case you might want to use it again.

- When drawing in your darts, you should true it by half an inch down from what you had mapped out from your pattern.

- Allow for seam lines when trying your pattern.

- Do not allow for a seam line at the center on your bodice.

Pros of Pinned-Pattern Method

1. You can easily modify your design or style while you drape.

2. You have a clear visualization of your design and what to expect at the end of your production.

3. You can truly express your skills and be very creative with your patterns.

4. There is a more precise fitting using this method.

Cons of Pinned-Pattern Method

1. It is time-consuming.

2. It is expensive.

3. You cannot eliminate the use of a form.

4. It cannot be used for commercial production.

5. It is mostly better used for designer clothing.

6. It requires different sizes of dress forms.

7. It requires lighter materials for draping.

Measurement Method

Also known as the Drafting method, this involves taking measurements of the individual that the cloth is being sewn for and cutting out drafts based on the measurement. You simply draw your patterns on paper based on the measurements that you have taken. Hence you have to ensure that you take precise measurements. A Block or Sloper can be utilized for a pattern draft. Basic blocks of patterns can be used from drafting, which includes bodice back, bodice front, skirt front, skirt back, and sleeves. These blocks can be added upon to create better designs.

Considerations when drafting

- Drafting should be done on a flat surface after the measurement has been taken.

- You should also carry out your drafting on the wrong side of the material.

- You should use the same size of paper required for the garment measurement.

- Ensure you use your French curves to make accurate curved lines.

- Distinguish back and front with different types of lines.

- Use your tailor's square to draw right angles.

- Well-sharpened pencils should be used for accuracy of lines.

Tools Required

- Paper (brown sheets)

- Pencil

- French curve

- Clear Ruler

- Measuring tape

What to consider when taking body measurements:

- **The posture of the individual-** Ensure that the person is standing erect when taking the measurement.

- **Remove all outer garments**- The person should take off any outer garments, especially jackets and coats that might alter the precise measurement that you intend to take.

- **Use quality tools**- Ensure you are using a quality standard measuring tape.

- **Round measure**- Take care to take round measurements in the arm areas, neck, and others. Don't let the tape be too tight or too slack.

Pros of measurement method

- A good draft can be easily graded to any size.

- You can easily get creative with basic blocks to get other designs for your choice.

- A draft can be stored up and used again and again.

- You can easily make corrections on the paper draft before cutting on the material.

- Wastage is less.

- It is inexpensive when compared to other methods.

Cons of Drafting

- It doesn't exactly fit all since the slopers are normally made based on the individual's body measured.

- A basic draft has no seam allowance but only ease; hence seam allowance is to be marked on the fabric.

What are Alterations?

Alteration is merely the act of making a change or modification on a garment or a pattern. In this section, we will be talking about pattern alterations.

Pattern alteration is adjusting a pattern to fit. There are many reasons why adjustments and alterations are often required in pattern making.

Most patterns might have been bought commercially: Commercial patterns are normally built with standard body sizes and frames. If you are one of those that buy commercial patterns for your production or for your personal use, then you will definitely need to understand alterations.

People want something unique: Whether you are designing something for yourself or for someone else, the chances are you might want something slightly different from a basic pattern or clothing.

Difference in body shape: Difference in body shapes can make you alter your own pattern, especially if you want to replicate the same pattern for another clothing for someone that might have a slight difference in size. Or, you may just want to alter the fit for yourself.

Difference in clothing preference and shape: You might have gotten tired of an old garment or style, and you want to redesign it to make something different; alterations would be just the thing that you need.

How I wanted to alter my trouser pattern

I'm a working mother, and I'm sure you can imagine the effort it takes to balance personal needs, my career, and my family. Honestly, one of my major personal goals has been to go back to having a flat tummy! Even though I am not exactly fat, I am just so psyched about a flat stomach. Oh, the shame I feel when I can't take in that bulge! It ruins the picture I would imagine in my mind as to how I want my clothes to look on me. But being who I am, I still try to hide it as much as I can with corsets, and the right pair of trousers. Sometimes, though, nobody wants to stifle their breathing or bring an amount of discomfort on themselves just because they have to wear a tummy trainer. That's why, if I ever get trousers, and they're not high-waisted, I have to alter them to my perfect fit, because that is the only way I can be comfortable in my clothes. Now, don't think I have thrown exercise to the wind, but it's just I haven't had the time! So, for now, I have to trust fitting my clothes to do my body trick for me, at least when I am all dressed up.

Importance/ Principles of Pattern Alteration

- **You should alter your pattern before cutting a garment**: Fitting alteration is important because once the fabric is cut, alteration or changes made are limited to the seam allowances and the darts on the garment. If you have a small allowance proportion you will be unable to carry out major changes on the garment; as such, you might be constrained to losing the already cut material.

- **Keep a record of pattern alterations**: Keeping record of pattern alterations is also important to help you go back to previously made changes or provide an opportunity to track the changes you have made.

- After a standard pattern alteration is done, you will observe that:

→ The designer line and design are preserved unless the design is purposely changed.

→ Changes are not obvious, and they do not affect other areas of the pattern.

→ The pattern remains flat and does not lose balance and proportion.

→ The grain lines are retained.

- **Corresponding patterns should also be altered**: The same pieces on the pattern must be altered to ensure that they correspond with the alterations of the major piece. For instance, the alteration made on your back bodice block should also be done on the front bodice block.

- **Add extensions with tape or glue**: Increases in length or width that have been added are made by taping or gluing the extension material (pattern tissue) to the original pattern.

- **Share the same structure as the original piece**: The altered pattern should have the same structure as the original pattern piece.

- **New altered pattern should be a flat block like the original pattern**: Ensure that your newly altered pattern retains the flat shape of the original block. This is because your block might tend to change in shape or fold if you don't follow the right principles or methods.

- Proper movement on altered lines to ensure that the altered line is the same as the original line.

- Ensure that you make slashes, folds, and adjustments parallel to the grain line. That is, parallel to the center front line or the center back line.

- When it comes to length and width, ensure that you make corresponding changes. On the other hand, this might not apply for alteration that has to do with increased bust area increase.

- Tucks and darts used to make width proportions smaller should be half of the actual amount removed.

- If an adjustment of the width is to be made when it comes to waist measurement, then divide the measurement to be added into two. And add the half-inch on one part of the pattern block and the other half on the other part.

To ensure that you have made all the right adjustments, here are some ways you can check your pattern to be certain you have made the right fit. You can use your mirror to check the adjustments before cutting your garment to ensure it is the right fit by placing it and the material area on your body or a form.

- → There is adequate ease for moving, sitting, and bending.

- → Grain lines that are crosswise are parallel to the floor.

- → The arms seam curves smoothly over the shoulder.

- → The crotch depth area is not too tight or too binding.

- → The darts made are pointing to the fullest parts of the curve made.

- → The hemline is even.

- → Your hipline is well fitted.

- → The side seams, center front, center back, and the lengthwise grain lines should hang straight or at right angle proportions to the floor.

- → The pants' legs hang smoothly and do not restrict the leg.

- → The waistband stays in place on the waist and fits when sitting and bending.

- → There is no excess fabric around or across the front or back crotch level.

- → The sleeves sit well, with no wrinkles.

Methods for Alterations

There are several methods. While it is almost impossible to achieve a perfect fit for most clothing without alterations, carrying out alterations with the wrong steps or the wrong way will cause a lot of problems for you and your fabric. Doing alteration the wrong way can lead to:

- → Wastage of fabric

- → Increased cost

- → Ruin of entire design and pattern

- → Waste of time

- → Dysfunctional design or dress

Fit is important to make garments achieve perfection, but sometimes perfection is subject to other factors. Here are some of the keys to a good fit:

Perfect measurement: Taking correct measurement is the foundation of all things. When taking measurements, try to ensure that it is done accurately.

Some best measurement practices includes:

Ensure that the individual stands up straight and looks forward at the time of the measurement. It can be a bit tricky taking floor-length measurement, particularly if you are taking it on your own body. So, if you are doing this for yourself, try to stand in front of the mirror and use a tape measure that you can simply allow to drop down and hang. This way, you don't have to bend to do your measuring.

When it comes to the breast area, our breast shape can vary in size when we are wearing a bra or not wearing a bra. If you are going to wear a bra with the finished garment, then take the measurements with you wearing a bra. Likewise, if you won't be wearing a bra, then leave it off when taking the measurements.

Trend: Trends, or the fashion outlook for the time, might be a bogus trend or a more eased-out pattern. This can be seen with tee-shirts or sweaters. Its style is not to hug the frame of the body, yet there must also be a fit to it. Hence, the pattern and alterations must fit the design that the trend is made for.

The elasticity of the fabric: This factor also affects alteration and is also looked at in our next chapter, "Fundamentals of Apparel Design." Alteration points will change depending on the type of fabric. You might need to allow and disallow an inch or less, based on the kind of fabric that you are using to make your finished work.

The amount of ease needed: Individuals might want different things in clothing production, especially when it comes to bespoke clothing. A standard way of making your design alteration might not play out when a person wants more room on her garment. This also means that this factor should be put into consideration when making alterations.

Size and type of figure: We all know that most of our bodies rarely fit into the standard image of a model. And when it comes to bespoke clothing for yourself, it can affect your pattern. Some persons might have more thigh proportions and more arm proportions than you would find in a model form. This makes alteration necessary. That might also affect other aspects of the pattern that has been designed. Taking this into account will help you choose the right alteration method. Commercial patterns are often prepared from standard body charts, so alteration on those patterns, if you want a bespoke fit, is inevitable. The methods of alteration might involve folding out excess areas to make the pattern block smaller. Or cutting through patterns to increase size and overlapping to decrease or increase dimension. Or by redrawing placement of dart and seams.

Below are the detailed methods of carrying out alterations.

Seam Method

Alteration using the Seam Method works great for adjustment on the seam lines and altering just along the grainline. Using a seam method works well if you are trying to adjust areas around the hip or waist for skirt, trouser, blouse patterns, and more.

It is quite easy to implement and allows you to make the changes on your pattern paper that you need so you can keep using it again and again. We will look at some simple steps to using the seam method in altering a pattern.

Material you need

→ Tissue paper

→ Your pattern to be adjusted

→ A pair of scissors

→ Some transparent tape

→ A clear ruler.

❑ **Step one**: Place the pattern on a flat surface, then identify the areas where you want to make alterations.

❑ **Step two**: Identify the pivot points. Remove the seam line. To expose the grainline, cut the pivot points to allow just enough to make a hinge.

❑ **Step three**: Place cardboard or paper underneath the area if you are making an additional adjustment.

❑ **Step four**: Then, you add the inches that are measurements that you intend to add to it. If you're making a reduction alteration, you can measure the area you will be cutting out, then when it is cut out, you can add your seamline back to your pattern by taping it back to the pattern.

Pivot Method

Also called the Pivot and Slide method, It is also a great way to make your pattern alterations. It focuses on working around the grain lines and allows you to make adjustments both on the width and length of your garment. I will be using a blouse pattern to show you how to use the pivot alteration method. In this project, we will be making alterations along the armhole. Most times, some standard blouse patterns might not conform to an individual's specific size, especially when it comes to the arm area, even when everything fits. Using Pivot for this saves the day.

Material you need

→ Tissue paper

→ Your pattern to be adjusted

→ A pair of scissors

→ Some transparent tape

→ A clear ruler.

→ Pins

❏ **Step one**: Place the pattern on a flat surface. Identify the areas where you want to make alterations. Place a pattern tissue underneath the pattern block that you are altering.

- ❏ **Step two**: Take the extra measurements that you will be adding and divide it by two.

- ❏ **Step three**: Use your pin to place it at the shoulder point where you will be taking the alteration from. When the pin is at that point, you can slide the pattern paper back and forth as you want. But do it just enough to measure out, and then mark the points of adding on your tissue.

- ❏ **Step four**: Join the points that have been marked with your pen or pencil.

- ❏ **Step five**: You can simply use glue to add your pattern, and it has been successfully adjusted.

You can also use the slide method to adjust the length of your basic pattern block. Add your new measurement and mark its points on the end of your tissue just beneath the pattern block. Simply slide the pattern block up to draw out and join the points that you have marked.

In pattern alteration and fitting, getting the grainline and structural line right is very important. After making or adjusting your pattern, this aspect of the pattern must be strongly considered to keep the fit in place. Using these methods of alterations ensure that your grainline and structural lines are in place to give your garment the actual design look it should have.

Chapter Summary

- Patterns are important in sewing because they help make sewing so much easier.

- There are several kinds of patterns; understanding types and methods of pattern-making is essential to making better clothes.

- Knowing the importance of alteration, and the many methods of alteration, will help you better understand why it is necessary to the sewing process.

In the next chapter, we will discuss the fundamentals of cloth design.

Chapter Three:
Fundamentals of Apparel Design

In apparel design, for you to create amazing designs and be at the top of your game as a designer, you must be willing to understand the concept of all areas of design and sewing before you can even begin. It's easy to think that a designer is one that simply sits down and drafts up creative illustrations for clothing on a notepad, but this is not the case. A designer would have to go through these fundamental steps we will be discussing in this book to have the kind of work that would produce successful clothing.

This chapter seeks to help those ready go through the process of understanding what it takes to create your own concepts, bring to life your own designs, and successfully showcase them to the world. As an alteration expert, you need to understand the methods of pattern-making, designs, and alterations. To make great alterations, you should understand design fundamentals.

These are fundamentals that affect everything. Without these basics, you might end up creating things that are not relevant or suitable. Remember that as a designer, what might appeal to you might not be appealing to the average person. While you might care about the details of your creation, like how you have managed to use a food theme to create a jumpsuit, someone else might only care about its fitting and trendiness.

As Vivienne Westwood said, "Fashion design is almost like mathematics; you have a vocabulary of ideas which you have to add and subtract in order to come up with an equation right for the times."

One of the strong factors that significantly affects the design we make is the trend. Historically, apparel has evolved to what we have today with each culture and age leaving its own little mark. So, how do you make your own design that someone would want to wear?

What *is* apparel? Apparel is clothing. Therefore apparel design is simply the act of designing clothing. This can range from garments, underwear, accessories, swimsuits, sportswear, and mostly whatever is worn on the body. As in all art forms, and also what we have always stated throughout this guide, it's vital to go back and understand design elements and principles.

Conceptualization of your Apparel Design

Developing your ideas for fashion should start with what you are designing, and who it's intended for. Well, if you are designing for yourself, the bridge might be quite narrow for you to cross, as you can simply do exactly whatever you have in mind. But, if you are conceptualizing ideas for a person that is not you, or for the public, you have to do much more.

Trends go as fast as they come, and trends are often not fair. Most fashion industry greats have gone on to set the trends over time. But how did they do this? What is a trend?

A trend could be defined as an aspect of popular culture - what everyone is doing now. To begin your design conceptualization, you must consider the trends, and if you want to set the trends, you should consider what makes them. Movies and shows are some of the things that have set trends socially. For example, the Moulin Rouge movie that influenced catwalk and fashion a few years ago.

You have to research fabrics, and read fashion guides and magazines to see designs from others. You can also learn from apparel design experts by studying about their works to understand how they conceptualize their designs. Some fashion firms sponsor their designers on trips to visit places to observe culture for inspiration. For a designer, absolutely anything can be an inspiration, and they should always be on the lookout.

They are always eager to see and feel something that might lead to a great creation. Some great designers have called singers or actors their muse, the person they gain inspiration from. You should always take your notepad with you to record, to draw, and take pictures when necessary.

Some people conceptualize with a theme. That approach creates a space with some boundaries, but where they can experiment with ideas that reflect the theme.

Creating your designs can be by drawing them or illustrating them. Designs are the foundation of a finished garment. Conceptualizing implies thinking about the design, and then you try to detail it with an image.

Drawing can be a difficult task, but just as in all arts, you must start with putting your first stroke down. You should preferably get a pencil and eraser for this. You may have a brilliant concept in your head, but if you never put it down on paper, we will never know if it would work or not!

Instead of worrying about the fact that it hasn't formed totally in your mind, you should go ahead and draw out the little bit you can imagine. If you have taken the first step of research correctly, then this won't be a problem. Your first draft, even if it's very raw, might form the basis for your best design yet.

What is the Difference between Illustration and Drawing?

Drawing simply portrays the schema of the clothing, while illustration creates an ambiance around the schema or structure of the design. This way, someone can know if the apparel can be worn in the summer or winter or how best you designed the outfit to be worn. You also get to know if this is for a lady in an office, a student, or just a teenage girl having fun. Illustrations can convey all these qualities.

This also brings us back to why researching is so important. When you know what matters in the industry, you can know if what you are doing has been done before. It also becomes easier to draw inspiration from already existing products. Many designers have drawn inspiration from military uniforms, for instance. Don't miss any opportunity to put down those strokes when an idea comes to mind.

Sketching Skills for Fashion Design

In drawing your design, it is important that your sketch portrays all the right proportions that you're trying to communicate. Not all of us are the best artists. But we can get better at it when we know a few steps and what to do exactly. Ensure you get a sharp hard pencil and a large blank notepad. You might also want to get some colored pens, but they're not vital, and you can usually get by without.

Scribbling something on paper and not getting it right can be a little disappointing. If you are like me, then it can make you feel like you don't belong in this design world after all. At least, that is what I felt when attempting to get through fashion school. I had a lot of ideas in my head, but I just didn't know how to translate them. I would be asked to try something, but I'd keep out of the way and hide behind others. There are people that are naturally confident with designs, and it almost feels like they were born for it, but that wasn't me. I wasn't a natural, and I mostly felt like the underdog. Nonetheless, I saw that, while it's effortless for some people, all I needed was practice, and I would be able to do well.

As with all industries and aspects of life, practice makes perfect. Talent is great, but it's not always enough; we all have to work at it. All skills and tactics possess steps and principles to getting things done. The underlying rule is that once those principles are put to work, you will get the expected result. This understanding gave me a foothold in my skill. So, you don't have to feel like you were born for this. If you put your mind to it, you can learn anything and be a professional at it.

It's the same thing with drawing; you can become good at it with these few steps.

You should start with creating a croquis on your notepad. This is a notepad model for your design. Some people would prefer getting on with their sketch without one. But this will help your design have form. You can draw a croquis that is standing straight or posing. Drawing one before sketching your design on it also helps you get the dress points right. A pose is often preferred, or even one that is kneeling. Whatever you think is appropriate and useful is fine. You should ensure that your lines are faint at this point.

Follow these simple steps to draw a Croquis

Even if you are bad at doing the sketches, these steps will help you draw out a pretty good croquis. Adding in your cloth sketch will become much easier.

What you will need

→ A clear sheet of paper

→ Sharp pencil

→ A ruler (A clear one preferably)

❑ **Step one**: Draw a straight line in the middle of your paper from the top to the bottom leaving small spaces on both ends.

❑ **Step two**: Divide the straight vertical lines drawn into nine places.

❑ **Step three**: Draw little horizontal lines on the line to mark the figure's areas.

❑ **Step four**: You can put little labels down and name them as follows; 1- Head, 2- Bustline, 3- Waist, 4- Hips, 5- Thighs, 6- Knees, 7- Calves, 8-Ankles. (These labels would automatically form what you draw at each of these points making it easy for you to form your croquis.)

❑ **Step five**: First, draw the head, making a circle on the first area from the head line above. Next, you draw the shoulders just below the head. Next you make a little horizontal line to draw the bustline, and, if you like, two small cups indicating bust.

- ❏ **Step six**: Draw out your waistline at the two ends to the point of the hip line and draw it down to your calves.

- ❏ **Step seven**: Next you make two circle points at your knee point, the calves point, and the ankle point.

- ❏ **Step eight**: Next you mark your crotch, just below the hip line. Draw two lines out from the crotch point to meet up at the ankles. You can draw some shoes at the floor point.

You can make out points for your eyes, nose, and mouth. Then, shade in some hair for your model.

When you are done with your croquis, you can now go ahead to draw your design clothing on it. You can also draw up your cloth lines by placing a transparent drawing sheet over the croquis sheet. On this sheet above it, you can easily see your croquis, so you can draw a better sketch of your dress or design on the form. That helps you make the right outlines that you need to make it what it should be.

Draw with faint lines and only begin to double your lines when you are sure that what you have drawn is what you want to be represented. This is so you can easily erase the pencil line if you get it wrong.

Once you are sure of your lines, you can begin to redraw your lines to emphasize your drawing or make them bold. Once this is done, you have created your perfect sketch.

Elements and principles of design

Elements of design

Elements of design are the basic qualities and aspects of the design process that form the ingredients of fashion. The clothes you are about to make are supposed to flatter people and make them ready for an evening ball. The different elements of design help you make proper design choices that would ensure that, while designing an apparel for an individual, you can focus on how to use these elements in the best ways that help enhance and flatter their best physical attributes.

Imagine trying to make designs for two different people with two distinct sizes. There is a slim petite lady and you also have a tall big lady. Your job is to make beautiful dinner gowns that would make them look stunning for the night. As you start on your design, you would have to first draw out your form and consider how this form would impact the look of your persona. You can think of sharp edges and round curves for your designs.

But the elements of design would help you understand who is better suited for a round curve and who is better suited for a straight edge. You can also consider bright colors, but you would also understand which element is better suited for a dark color than who is better suited for a bright color. Ever wondered why Adele likes black? Maybe that's just because her designer knows what's best for her. Remember that the goal of design is to flatter the best parts of the persona.

- **Form**: Also called the shape or silhouette, it is the comprehensive outline of your apparel. This forms how the whole garment is seen. This creates the total impact of what the garment is and what it represents.

The shape of the apparel is meant to compliment the shape of the individual's body or compliment their best parts. It is the form of the clothing that you notice when it is being looked upon. It is the form that tells you if the person is wearing a jacket or a shirt or a gown. The form is very important. Some aspects are the type of fabric and method of design and construction on the shape or form of your final garment. The shape of garments continue to evolve as trends change to further and better highlight the form of an individual.

- ➢ **Line**: Lines are visually expressive. Lines can make a person appear shorter, taller, slimmer, or fatter. Edges are important; these edges can be both within and without the clothing but they are significant in how the garment is seen and formed.

The lines on an apparel are seen as the cuts and seemingly style lines that are created when making an apparel. These lines often work as the element of your design that creates the kind of visual impact that one might see in a dress. Lines on an apparel can make the individual look thinner or fatter. Or you have some features of the body being flattered more than other areas. Lines create shapes like you have for your pleats and darts, especially when it comes to design patterns. It creates more visuals for the blouse then you find on a basic bodice.

Lines can be curved, straight, and structural. Whether diagonal, vertical, or horizontal, these all fall under straight lines. Straight lines work to decrease or increase width or height. Straight diagonal lines that are short are normally seen in jackets, or bell-bottom trousers; the lines would decrease the width of your apparel.

Curved lines will add to the fullness of the apparel. While a curved line adds to the roundness you are trying to portray in a design sketch, when used to illustrate your folds, a more flattened out curve on the apparel gives the body more form representation therefore is considered more flattering. Rounder curves would make your apparel appear fuller.

Structural lines are those kinds of lines that make up the form or structure of the apparel. The structural lines that appear on most garments are the darts and the seam. This is responsible for the fitting and structure of the apparel. There are order lines that are mostly designed for decorative purposes but these are not structural lines. These can be made just to accentuate a certain style or area of the apparel.

- **Color**: Colors are one of the most important elements of a design. They translate to the perception of the finished garment and can influence body structure when mixed with texture. However, on their own, colors can be used as one sees fit with respect to the design and other characteristics. Color describes how fun or cool the apparel looks.

- **Texture**: The texture of an apparel is the perceived nature or quality of it. People can use different sensory organs to perceive the structure. You can decipher with your eyes that someone is wearing a satin fabric, for instance. The texture of an apparel largely influences the apparel. This represents the hardness and softness of a fabric. A fabric that is soft or light will drape differently than would a heavy fabric. This is why fabric like satin would fall more easily on the body than leather or thick clothing.

A satin fabric would also show the edges of the body more than cotton fabric would. Hence, you would discover that an older male, for instance, might not feel most comfortable in clothing made from satin. You would also find that there are fabrics which hide the brightness of colors that other fabrics would bring out. If you had a bright blue crepe, it would come out differently than someone wearing a satin blue. You can begin to imagine that bright-colored satin clothing would look a lot more flattering on a slim person than a chubby person.

Design Principles

Design principles are the ideals that help you and guide you in the application of the element of the design. In Apparel design our goals are mainly to accentuate the best physical aspects of the person, achieve reasonable comfort for the person, and improve and portray a beautiful physical appearance of the individual. Using design principles as a guide would help you use your elements wisely in ensuring that you achieve these goals.

- **Balance**: The balance in a design can be asymmetrical or symmetrical. An asymmetric design means that the design is not balanced on both sides. This means that the weight of the design is not evenly distributed at both ends. This can be seen on a dress where there are different cuts at the ends of the skirt.

An example might be a short-long design. Symmetric apparels are normally seen in a formal apparel where there is an even cut at both ends, so we can say that the fabric is evenly distributed. Designs can also have emphasis where you have created a focus in certain areas of the design. This can bring more attention to that area, while also removing attention from other areas.

- ➢ **Rhythm**: Rhythm in a design is created where there is a flow with the colors and the cuts on the design. This can be best seen where color patterns are well-distributed. Or, in cases where different kinds of fabric are used, it is well-distributed and is balanced across the apparel. This also applies for the distribution of the lines used for decoration.

- **Unity**: Unity of design is achieved when one can see that design all falls into place as one. Each part of the elements come together to create and portray one single effect , theme, or style.

Fabric and Technique

Having an understanding of fabric types and the nature of fabric is very important. The fabric you choose will affect the drape, the fitting and comfort of the fabric. This in turn affects the general turn out of your fabric.

Getting used to as many fabric names and characteristics as you can will help you choose the right fabric that best portrays the effect of the design you want to put out. For instance a heavy material for pleats would come out different than a lighter material. Fabrics also affect the fit of your design a lot.

Whatever you are designing, you would strongly have to take into account the kind of fabric. Some fabric stretches. As such, when designing your pattern, you would have to take that into consideration. Fabrics that stretch would fit differently than fabrics that don't. You would have to account for the stretch when taking your measurements. This is typically seen on denim jeans and on leggings. Even though they both fit, they do not have the same area because the leggings have a stretch characteristic. If the leggings were designed with the same size of pattern as the jeans then perhaps it would look poor on you.

The fabric will have an affect on the technical aspect of your design.

➢ **The Opacity**: Depending on the fabric you use, you may require a lining to bring out the desired result you expect from your production. Also if it is a sheer fabric, you would need a lining to reduce transparency. This would have to be taken into account when stitching and preparing your pattern.

➢ **The kind of stitches and seams to be used**: If the fabric stretches, or has more weight, you would have to use a stitch that gives more to avoid thread breakage. You would also choose a different kind of stitching for a stronger hold depending on the weight of the fabric.

➢ **The size of your garment:** Some fabrics are narrower than others. The size of your garment would make you want to lay your fabric side-by-side to accommodate required size if it is a fabric with narrow width. This might also affect the size and nature of your pattern. Hence, it is advisable to understand the kind of pattern you would be using when designing before creating your pattern.

> **Shrinkage**: Shrinkage mostly happens after the clothing is made. And some fabric will shrink with time. If you require ironing during your pre-production process, it might end up getting folded or squeezed in some areas.

> **Fabric handling**: The kind of fabric would also affect fabric handling if you are doing a commercial production. Even when it is a bespoke outfit, you would need to set out handling processes that would ensure you don't donate the fabric. Also, the right tools should be used to avoid breakage or wearing out of tools.

Textiles

Textiles are made from a combination of thin threads, or yarns or filaments or fibres that are either obtained naturally or artificially or a combination of both. They are made by weaving, knitting, or felting. Combining is interlocking these lengths of fibers or threads in different prescribed patterns to make up a cloth used for sewing. The different properties of fiber affect the final product of the cloth made.

- Silk: Silk is made naturally from silkworms. There are a lot of other animals that produce silk, for textile production it is mostly made from silkworms. It has a long history through countries like India and China. It is known for its soft and durable nature. It is the strongest natural fiber in the world. Silk continues to be a popular fiber because of its cultural and historic heritage. There are now synthetic alternatives for natural silk, but silk is still naturally harvested in some parts of the world. It is mostly used for blouses, nightgowns, evening gowns, and the like.

- Cotton: Cotton is a natural fabric. It is a textile made from the natural cotton plant. It is an insoluble organic compound. It is harvested and spun into yarn, which is then woven into cotton fabric that creates soft cotton clothing. Cotton is commonly the first choice when it comes to fabrics for bedding, underwear, and everyday apparel because it's soft and affordable. Linen is made from cotton.

- Damask: Damask is a fabric with patterns that are woven and not printed on. The designs are achieved with the use of satin weave. Damask fabric can be made with different textiles like satin, linen, wool.

- Cashmere: This is a type of textile obtained from natural sources. It is known for its softness and comfortable feel. It is a type of wool made from cashmere goats and pashmina goats. It is very fine and soft to touch. Mostly, it has a light feel like silk. Sometimes it is blended with other types of wool to give it a heavy feel.

- Canvas: Canvas is a type of textile that is plain-weave made out of heavy cotton yarn. It is a sturdy hard textile. It is known for being durable and strong. It can become a strong outdoor fabric and even water-resistant when you blend cotton with synthetic fibres.

- Chenille: Chenille can be made from materials like cotton, silk, wool, or rayon. Chenille is also the name for the type of yarn used.

- Crepe: This is a fabric that was traditionally made from silk, Crepes can be thin, thick, or lightweight; they mostly look like they have a crinkled dull surface. They are used for evening gowns and some home decors because of how they drape. It is also made from silk or wool or both; today, it can also be made from other synthetic fibers.

- Linen: This is a lightweight and extremely strong fabric. It is made from the flax plant. Linen dries faster than cotton. It is a breathable fabric, and is used to make inner linings of clothing on jackets and other garments. However, it wears out with washing and ironing. It has poor elasticity hence it wrinkles quickly. It is easy to clean. It is more biodegradable than cotton.

- Satin: Satin is a weave that is used to create many kinds of fabrics. Fabrics that are characteristic of satin weave are mostly also called satin or have names accompanied with satin. Satin is used to make nightgowns, lingerie, men's underwear, and also pointe shoes for ballet. If satin weave is used with filament fibers such as silk, polyester, and nylon, the resulting fabric is known as satin. It is a rather soft, shiny, and glossy fabric on its front and has a dull looking back.

Chapter Summary

- Never forget the four basic elements of design. They are the foundation on which you learn to make your first cut.

- The three principles of design discussed in this chapter will guide you in the application of the elements of the design.

- An understanding of the different types of fabric available will help you learn to work with other materials. You should be able to make the right patterns for a cloth if you know how these materials act and respond.

In the next few chapters, you will learn how to make some patterns.

Chapter Four:
Project I – Redesign a Man's Long Shirt Into a Woman's Beautiful Dress

In this first project, we are going to start with redesigning a man's long shirt. There is so much you can do with alterations when trying to design old clothes or already made clothing. This project is not intended to restrict you to this form of redesigning; rather, it is just an example to help you try new ideas.

Using a man's long shirt to be transformed into a woman's dress, we can redesign this into a halter neck gown or an off-shoulder dress, or a plunge neck dress. We can basically do whatever we want with this shirt and have very few restrictions. (Note that depending on your design, you might have to add more fabric to achieve what you have in mind.) In this project, we will be making a plunge-neck women's dress with a waist belt. Let's get started!

Tools needed:

> → A sewing machine

> → A meter rule

> → A pencil or any other marking tool

> → A pair of scissors

→ Some pins

→ A man's long shirt

If you already have a sketch of what you want to achieve, then that would be fine, but if you don't, then you might want to draw a sketch of what you want to accomplish. Then, you can follow the pattern in achieving that design. So, if you do, then your design should be in front of you in the same way that I always have mine in front of me.

❏ **Step one**: Your long shirt should be dressed in a form, but if you don't have one, you can simply wear it in front of the mirror and begin to take your markings. First, you take your pencil and take your markings on the arm/sleeves of the shirt. You mark how far you want the sleeves of the shirt to get to.

❏ **Step two**: Cut off the sleeves of the shirt at the line that you have marked.

❏ **Step three**: Normally, you would take the shirt and place it on a flat surface. If you had placed it on a form, you could simply do all your alterations on the form. Next, you use your pencil or tailor's chalk to mark around the collar and the area you want to have the plunge of the neckline. Then, you make your cutting along that line.

❑ **Step four:** You bring the sleeves you have
previously cut and cut out vertical pieces of
fabric from the sleeves. They will form the
waist belt that is about to be made.

Once you have cut out all these, you're ready to
start making your woman's long dress. Turn out your
dress and put it back on the form. Then, you fold
along the line you have cut, just little folds, and begin
to use your pins to tack around it. You will do so for
the arm area, and for the neck plunge area. Take your
pinned-up fabric to the sewing machine and start
sewing the folded areas. Once you are done with this,
take the cut-out fabric for the belt and sew round the
edges.

Once you have done this, you are ready to try on
your plunge dress with a waist belt on. You can also
decide to add hems to the sleeves to decorate your
dress further. Congratulations! You have successfully
transformed your man's long shirt into a woman's
beautiful dress.

Chapter Five:
Project II – Combine Two Different Color Tee-Shirts Into One

In this next project, we will be combining two different colors of tee-shirts into one. Plain tee shirts are boring, so we want to add some fun to it. This project is a very fun one, and it's a great one to embark on if you are just starting with alteration projects.

You can put together pattern print shirts of two different patterns, or put together stripe shirts of two different stripe colors, or also to try out just plain-colored shirts together. This project is very flexible, and you can choose to do it for male or female tee-shirts. Whatever kind of shirt you choose to work with here, these steps still will work effectively for you. Let's get started! In this project, we will be putting together or combining two different color tee-shirts into one, and two different collared striped shirts into one.

What is needed?

> → Sewing machine

> → Pair of Scissors

> → Seam ripper

→ Pins

→ Rotary cutter

→ Tailor's chalk

→ Two shirts to combine

❑ **Step one**: Get the two shirts that you would want to combine. You should ensure that the shirt is of the same length and width as the other one. You might want to do something that has the same designs on it or maybe try alternate designs. If you would be doing a shirt with a collar, as in the striped collared shirt we are doing side by side, you would also need to get a collared shirt with the same length and width as each other.

❑ **Step two**: For the tee-shirt, all you have to do is fold the shirt into two equal parts right at the middle and cut in between from the neck to the bottom. Do the same for the second shirt. For the collared shirt, you would first need to use your seam ripper to rip the seams at the collar to take the collars off the shirt.

You would need to remove the collars for the two shirts that you would be combining. Then, you turn the shirt to its back and ensure it is equally folded into two to start cutting. Ensure that you get a straight line.

❑ **Step three**: Both for the tee-shirt and the collared shirt, bring the two different parts together that have been cut, alternate them into the back side of the shirt, then use your pins to pin up the shirts to hold them together.

❑ **Step four**: Once you have held them together, then you can take them to your sewing machine and start sewing.

❑ **Step five**: For both shirt edges, you can decide to do an optional zigzag sewing on the edges of the shirt where you made the center cut for durability of the clothing before placing it on the flat surface to start pinning them together. After this, you can head to your sewing machine to sew together the fabric you have pinned together. Once this is done, your tee-shirt is ready to go. But for your collared shirt, there are still a few more steps to take.

❑ **Step six**: Take your sleeved shirt and fit into the collar of the shirt. You can choose to take any of the collars of the shirt you most prefer. You can also decide to take out the pocket from the other shirt and place it on the alternate one.

There you have it! You should have successfully combined a two-colored tee-shirt and a long-sleeved collared shirt into one garment.

Chapter Six:
Project III- Alter Your Low Waist Jeans to High Waist

This next project is one of my favorite projects to do, especially as a DIY project. In this chapter, we will be altering low waist jeans to high waist jeans. If you've read some previous chapters in this guide, you'll understand that I tend to go for high waist jeans!

High waist jeans are so much more comfortable, especially for people like me who do not do so well in the flat tummy area. Even for those who have terrific figures, it's always a great way to enhance your hips curve and accentuate your slender waist. The high waist look effortlessly flatters your figure. Now, let's get started altering your low waist jeans into high ones.

Materials you need

- → Sewing machine

- → Seam rippers

- → A pair of scissors

- → Measuring tape or a meter rule

- ❏ **Step one**: Spread out your low waist jeans that you are about to adjust into high waist jeans. If you have particular jeans which you would like your low waist jeans to be like, then you can also spread out those jeans to take a measurement from them.

- ❏ **Step two:** Take the crotch measurement from the already existent high waist jeans and record it.

- ❏ **Step three**: Rip out the seams on the crotch line of the low waist seam. You can simply rip the threads out until it gets to a considerable length where you know that your already measured crotch length will get to.

- ❏ **Step four**: Straighten the areas you have loosened. Then, you take the measurement to check if it's the same with your already recorded measurement for your high waist. Cut out the extra areas you have made. Be careful not to cut too much, so it doesn't become too tight.

- ❏ **Step five:** Once you get the exact measurement, use tailor's chalk to make that point. Then you use your pins to hold the seams, back and front of the length you have opened up.

- ❏ **Step six**: Begin to stitch it up.

Once you've stitched it up, then you have successfully redesigned your low waist jeans into high waist jeans. Go ahead, and put them on to be sure they fit you perfectly.

Chapter Seven:
Project IV – Make a Simple Pattern of Male Trousers

Trousers are one of the most common clothing essentials, especially male trousers. There is almost no male on earth without at least a pair of trousers. This gives you a good idea how popular they are. However, they can be a bit tricky to create. Making patterns for trousers takes a bit more care than your basic pattern making.

You can think of tight trousers like skinny jeans, or you can think of trousers like plain trousers. Or possibly just well-fitted pants. Whatever your specific need might be, you can tailor your male trouser pattern to look exactly like what you want them to be with these basic steps we will be sharing. Let's get started.

Materials you need:

→ Pattern paper/ dotted paper

→ Scissors

→ Pencil

→ Measuring tape

→ Curved ruler

→ Pattern master/meter rule

→ Clear rule

→ Glue/tape

❑ **Step one**: Spread out your pattern paper or dotted paper on a flat surface. You should either cut out an amount of paper that you know will be sufficient for this project based on the measurement or size of the individual or form that you have taken. Or, simply roll out some of your paper and only cut after you have taken measurement.

❑ **Step two**: Take measurements. These are the following measurements that you should take;

I like to streamline the measurements to take in making trouser patterns into two.

- *The horizontal measurements*

- *The vertical measurements.*

For the vertical measurements, we start out taking the measurements from the waist.

Use your measuring tape to take measurements for the following areas,

→ Your waist down to your hip.

→ Your waist down to your crotch (also called the crotch depth measurement). This is taken from your waist to the end of your bottom when you are seated.

→ Your waist to your knee

→ Your waist to your ankle

For the horizontal measurements, we start out taking the following measurements:

→ Your waist measurement, by wrapping the tape around your waist.

→ Your hip measurement (the tape should be placed around the middle of your buttocks region).

→ Your knee measurement

→ Your ankle measurement

❑ **Step three**: Write down all your measurements because you need them to draft your pattern.

❑ **Step four**: Make a vertical line on your pattern paper using your pencil. Then, make another horizontal line joining it at the top.

❑ **Step five**: Mark out your waist to hip, waist to crotch, waist to knee, and waist to ankle.

❑ **Step six**: You can either use your clear ruler or pattern master for this. Place your clear ruler on your vertical line and mark out (use your pencil to simply shade or tick the area) the measurement you have taken off your waist to hip area. This would be the area from the top of your waistline at the top of the vertical line to where your measurement of your waist to hip line ends. Also, mark out your waist to crotch, waist to knee, and waist to ankle in the same way.

❑ **Step seven**: Place your clear ruler horizontally from the vertical line where you had earlier marked your hip point and draw out a horizontal line to mark out your hip measurement line. For instance, if my hip measurement is 7inches, I will draw out a horizontal 7 inches from the beginning of the vertical line to where 7 inches ends. Also, draw out a horizontal line to mark your waist measurement (your waist measurement is the line that you drew at the top. Hence, it is already drawn. All you have to do is to mark it), mark your knee measurement and ankle measurement.

❑ **Step eight**: Divide your hip measurement into four. Place your clear ruler on the point where your hip measurement stops and draw out another horizontal line to the point where your hip measurement, divided by four, would end.

- ❏ **Step nine**: take your curved ruler or French curve to join the point you just drew out to connect to the line connecting your hip to your waist point.

- ❏ **Step ten**: Make your darts by drawing a line from the point of your crotch line divided by four to your waistline. Measure 4 and ½ inches from your waistline down to your hip line. Mark that point on the centerline you have previously drawn. Connect both lines. (An average dart goes 4 and ½ inches down your center front.)

- ❏ **Step eleven**: divide your thigh measurement, your hip measurement, and draw down.

- ❏ **Step twelve**: measure the horizontal ankle line and mark it where it ends and the beginning point. Then, use your pattern master to draw from that point up to your thigh line. At this point, you have succeeded in creating most of the front side of your trouser pattern. What is left at this stage is adding your seam allowance and recreating your pattern from the back side.

- ❏ **Step thirteen**: place another pattern paper, or in our case, a dotted paper above your drafted pattern (I prefer a dotted paper because it is lighter and you can easily trace your work into the new paper). Begin to trace your drafted pattern on the new pattern on it. You can use a tracing wheel for this before you begin using a pencil to bold it, or you can go right ahead and use a pencil to trace out what is already done underneath.

❑ **Step fourteen**: Mark out the same lines you have made. Cut out excess paper around.

❑ **Step fifteen**: Create your seam allowance around it (Standard seam allowance is between half an inch to an inch), depending on what the pattern maker prefers. In my case, I prefer half an inch. You create your seam allowance by measuring out half an inch on all the surrounding areas you have drawn out and adding a parallel line to it. You can cut out more of the excess paper to allow for only your newly-made pattern.

Another way you can replicate your pattern, if you were using a pattern paper, is to place the other pattern paper at the back of it and make it lap properly with a tap. Then you begin to cut through the edges to achieve a second replicate. After this, you can now also use a tracing wheel to achieve the lines and measurements that are on your top pattern paper.

Note that this is a basic fit trouser. If you want to make skinny pants or more fitted trousers, you would have to reduce the width around the thigh to ankle.

That is your basic Male Trouser Pattern! You can now cut out your pattern and cut out the material you want to sew.

Chapter Eight:
Project V - Create a Blazer Pattern

Blazers are normally stand-alone clothing, and, most times, you think of a blazer as a jacket that is worn by men and women. A blazer, however, has distinctive features that come with it, and this should be considered when creating or designing a pattern for one. It can be worn over trousers or shorts and would normally come with distinct buttons. Standard blazers have sharp shoulders and come together on the waist area; they drape down a bit close to the crotch level.

Some blazers are made with hard materials like leather, and, in most cases, a lining is also added. All this should be taken into consideration when making your pattern.

Also, the lapels are a very important part of a blazer. Wearing a blazer creates a sort of casual appearance in a normal setting, and it is a nice way to blend into both informal and formal crowds if you are trying to play safe. In this project, we will be creating a blazer.

What you would need

> → Pattern paper
>
> → A sharp pencil

→ Pattern Master/ Meter ruler

→ Eraser

→ Pen

→ Tracing wheel

→ A basic bodice pattern block

In creating a blazer pattern, we would be working with a basic bodice block to make our blazer pattern. In the previous chapter, we have talked about making a basic bodice block. So you can refer to the preceding chapter to make one. Now, to get started,

- ❏ **Step one**: Spread out your bodice block on another pattern paper that you have spread out on a flat surface.

- ❏ **Step two**: Trace around your basic bodice to create the same block on your new pattern paper. Connect the lines to your waist and sleeves. Add lengths from the waist down if you want your blazer to be longer, which should be the case.

- ❏ **Step three**: Mark one inch out of your waistline. This should be where your button would be placed, depending on the design of your blazer.

- ❏ **Step four**: Draw a line from your line to the hem. Draw the curve from where the arm line is and join it.

- ❏ **Step five**: Make the revere collar- mark half of your back neckline measurement and connect to the front.

- ❏ **Step six**: Mark one inch away from the center front and draw a line.

- ❏ **Step seven**: Add facing and lines for the lining.

- ❏ **Step eight:** Take your newly-completed blazer pattern and place on another clear pattern paper to make the front block of it. After which, you transfer to your material and start stitching.

Chapter Nine:
VI - Ladies' Blouse Pattern and Experimenting with Sleeves

Blouses are an essential part of ladies' clothing. They're worn over skirts and trousers. They have been around for a long time in different styles and forms. One of the essentials of a lady's blouse is the bodice frame, which covers the neckline and the armhole, with all the other upper-body measurements taken into consideration. It should be able to accentuate the waist and the bust, while nicely complementing a skirt or trousers, depending on the design that you are adopting.

A ladies' blouse pattern is much like a basic bodice pattern, which you can now do so much with. In this project, we will be first creating the blouse pattern, after which we will be creating patterns that different sleeves would be added to.

Materials you would need:

- → Set Square

- → Tape measure

- → Pattern master

- → Pattern paper

- → Pencil

To make your blouse pattern, there are some measurements that you should take.

→ The upper bust area

→ The bust line

→ The waistline

→ The hip line

→ The space between the two nipples (for your darts)

❏ **Step one**: Spread out your pattern paper on a flat surface. And make a straight line, or in this case, we would be using the edge of the pattern paper as the centerfold.

❏ **Step two**: Measure out and mark the bustline, the upper bust line, the waistline, and the hip line from the centerfold line (that is the vertical edge of the pattern paper).

❏ **Step three**: Draw out your horizontal lines to the points that you have marked.

❏ **Step four**: Insert your waist darts by dividing your nipple to nipple point measurement into two. Create your darts by drawing a line that starts one inch below the bust line and two inches above the hip line.

❏ **Step five**: Draw out your arm length.

❏ **Step six:** Draw out your neck length and your neck back length.

That is your blouse pattern. Now, we would be following the next steps to create and experiment with a few sleeve patterns on this blouse pattern. There are so many types of sleeves that can be attached to blouses. You can get so many blouse patterns depending on the kind of design that you have created. Here are steps to make a standard sleeve for a blouse.

Take measurements of:

→ Your sleeve length

→ Around your bicep

→ Around your elbow

→ Around the wrist

→ Your arms

❏ **Step one**: Spread out your pattern paper on a flat surface.

❏ **Step two**: Draw a straight line; mark your sleeves length.

❏ **Step three**: Mark your bicep width on the line, mark the elbow, and the wrist width. Join the lines (that is making horizontal lines from the sleeves length).

❑ **Step four:** Mark the midpoint of your bicep width. Draw a line up from the midpoint of your bicep.

❑ **Step five**: Connect the wrist point to the end of the bicep line. Divide the front line slant by four. Mark the points around the slant to make the top sleeve curve.

Your sleeve pattern is normally down for both sides. Even though it can seem complicated, it is so easy, that, when it's done, you can always use it again and again, only making necessary adjustments.

Chapter Ten:
Project VII – Create Six Types of Collar (3 Women and 3 Men)

Collars are a very important part of clothing. In many garments, collars are more than just decoration. Collars found on the neck area of garments both for females and males have now become so important that there are very few garments that don't have one.

Apart from the stylish look they give, collars are also very functional. For instance, they can serve as neck warmers and help reduce cold in chilly parts of the world. It also helps keep the armor from chafing and helps reinforce the neck ends of your fabric to avoid ripping.

There are different kinds of collars. Some can be standing, while others are folded. Irrespective of the type, a standard collar should:

- Embrace the neckline.

- It should be free of any wrinkles.

- It should have smooth curves or sharp points depending on the type or style of the collar.

- It should be interfaced in the right way to retain shape.

- The stitching along the outer seam edge should be stitched in such a way as to make sure that it's not visible.

- The collar should be well-pressed.

- The collar should be graded to reduce thickness.

Basically, you will be creating patterns to conform to the collar you want to make.

Here are the basic kinds of collars for male and female.

For Females, we have:

The Revere Collar: this kind of collar is mostly used for jackets, blazers, or suit jackets. They are normally bigger in size and tend to flatten out at the back; then they merge with a lapel.

Turtle neck Collar: This can be long or short, depending on the style of the design. They are normally standing collars for females, but, overall, in designs today, they are used for both men and women.

Peter Pan Collar: This is a curved flat collar that falls completely on the dress.

Creating Collar patterns

Materials you will need:

→ A sharpened pencil

→ A basic bodice pattern

→ A pattern paper

→ A clear ruler

→ A tracing wheel

→ A measurement of the collar width that you want to make

The Peter Pan Collar

❑ **Step one**: Take out the basic bodice pattern and spread on a flat surface. Place another pattern paper under the basic bodice and trace out the back neckline and the armhole.

❑ **Step two**: Take your basic bodice front and also place it on the flat surface. Then make your front bodice block and your back bodice block to meet shoulder-to-shoulder. This should form a C- curve. Also, trace out the C-curve, the armhole of the front basic bodice.

❑ **Step three**: Use your width measurement to mark points from the end of the neck around the neckline.

❑ **Step four**: Make a curve using the points that you have marked.

❑ **Step five**: Add another 0.25 cm to hide your seams.

- ❑ **Step six**: Add notches to the front area of your collar.

- ❑ **Step seven**: Cut out your pattern to begin sewing.

The Turtle Neck Collar

- ❑ **Step one**: Take out the basic bodice pattern and spread it on a flat surface. Place another pattern paper under the basic bodice and trace out the back neckline and the armhole.

- ❑ **Step two**: Take your basic bodice front and also place it on the flat surface. Use your width measurement to mark points from the end of your neck to how high you want your turtle neck to get to.

- ❑ **Step three**: Draw the line from your neck curve to meet the point you have marked.

- ❑ **Step four**: Use your curved ruler to curve the end of the neckline connecting to the newly ruled line so as to make a curve.

- ❑ **Step five**: Add another 0.25 cm to hide your seams.

- ❑ **Step six**: Add notches to the front area of your collar.

❑ **Step seven**: cut out your pattern to begin sewing.

The Revere Collar

❑ **Step one**: Take out the basic bodice pattern and spread it on a flat surface. Place another pattern paper under the basic bodice and trace out the back neckline and the armhole.

❑ **Step two**: First, design your lapel by marking the lines in front of the bodice length.

❑ **Step three:** Take your basic bodice front and also place it on the flat surface. Mark a line on top of your neckline; that would join your neckline to make your reverse collar.

For males, we have:

The Open Sport Collar

The open sport collar is normally for a man's sport shirt. These shirts are mostly buttoned up.

❑ **Step one**: Take out the basic bodice pattern and spread it on a flat surface. Place another pattern paper under the basic bodice and trace out the back neckline and the armhole.

❑ **Step two**: First, design your lapel by marking the lines in front of the bodice length.

- ❑ **Step three**: Take your basic bodice front and also place it on the flat surface. Mark a line on top of your neckline; that would join your neckline to make your sports collar.

The Mandarin Collar

The mandarin collar sits around the neck on formal men's clothing. Follow these steps to draft the collar.

- ❑ **Step one:** Take out the basic bodice pattern and spread it on a flat surface. Place another pattern paper under the basic bodice and trace out the back neckline.

- ❑ **Step two**: Measure and mark out the points of the mandarin collar. If you want it standard, you should ensure that you measure just one inch. If you want it longer, you should increase it by half an inch higher.

- ❑ **Step three:** Mark the seam allowances on your neckline. Measure from the center back to the shoulder line. Then measure from the centre front to the front shoulder line.

- ❑ **Step four**: Connect the points you have marked, and draw your lines to connect from the beginning of center back and the center front to the measured area.

❏ **Step five:** Add ¼ inch around the lines connected to form your seam lines and cut out your mandarin collar pattern.

The Square Collar

To draft the square collar, follow the steps below,

❏ **Step one**: Take out the basic bodice pattern and spread it on a flat surface. Place another pattern paper under the basic bodice and trace out the back neckline.

❏ **Step two**: Measure and mark out the points of the square collar.

❏ **Step three**: Mark the seam allowances on your neckline. Measure from the center back to the shoulder line. Then, measure from the center front to the front shoulder line.

❏ **Step four**: Connect the points you have marked, and draw your lines to connect from the beginning of center back and the center front to the measured area.

❏ **Step five**: Cut out the square Collar Pattern.

Once they're created, you can easily fit your collars on your neckline. Collars continue to be an irreplaceable aspect of most clothing.

Conclusion

Pattern making is a very important aspect of apparel design, fitting, and alterations. You can do nothing of significance without these attributes. Great pattern-makers become so with years of experience and usually continue to teach others.

In this guide, we have established that, with diligence and great eye for detail, there's nothing stopping you from creating some of the world's best designs. The only ceiling is your imagination and creativity.

Even though there are so many beautiful designs today, why shouldn't the future be draped with inventions that only you can imagine?

We have also established that understanding the fundamentals will guide you into making the right choices. You'll learn the right way to design and make alterations for the best fit.

Those who have done it in the past, and have laid the groundwork for us today, discovered that apparel designing was not just their career but their vocation.

Some famous pattern designers include:

Alexander McQueen

Alexander Mcqueen was the chief fashion designer at Givenchy from 1996 to 2012, after which he started his label. He became one of the major designers of the 21st Century and has made his mark in the fashion industry with his work in Givenchy. He was very innovative, often disruptive, and continued to break rules and present new ideas. He designed the armadillo heels and the low waisted trend of the time. Some critics even called him the hooligan of fashion as he continued to create over-the-top designs. His designs were also notable for their precision and detailed touch.

He often draped on models and started from the side to cut. According to him, this was to ensure that all the curves and lumps were dealt with precisely, and nothing was missed out. One of his other notable designs recently is the Misses/Misses' petite jumpsuit. This is loose on the waist, straight-legged, has shoulder pads, a side zip, and side buttons. This pattern was embraced by professional and home sewers alike. His collections also carried lots of silhouettes. His approach has featured wide neck dresses with a combination of different fabrics to transcend trends.

Stella McCartney

The daughter of one of the world-famous Beatles, Stella McCartney is an English fashion designer. She has continued to impress the world of fashion since 1995. Her clean-cut garments continue to give her an edge, especially when it comes to women's wear, from everyday clothes to dinner apparel. She has designed ladies' bags, sneakers, and jewelry. She campaigns for animal rights; her clothes are not made with fur or leather. Her best pieces are feminine, comfortable, and sharp. Her styles range from ankle cut pants to blazers and coats. She loves to use bright colors and soft fabrics.

Phoebe Philio

Former creative director of Celine, Phoebe Philio has been a big name in the fashion industry. Her designs are a reflection of her Northern English heritage since she focuses on designs for working-class women; clothes that are chic, classy, and comfortable. Phoebe's work is suitable for office apparel and an evening out.

Alexander Wang

Alexander Wang is one of the major designers in fashion today. His styles are embraced by both old and young. They are mostly ready-to-wear, plus comfortable women's and men's wear. His shirt-like design that forms a skirt that buttons down while the sleeves tie in front is especially chic and fun. His 2015 winter collection also broke boundaries with unusual button positions and spiraling zippers. Classic tailoring pieces were reinvented to have the crotch area redesigned to the back, and included top-stitched shaped pockets. His designs have reinvented female wear and have been resonant, comfortably competing with some of the big names of fashion.

Marc Jobs

Marc Jacob is an American fashion designer who became prominent after designing men's wear and swimwear for years under his own brand. He has created styles that have stormed the red carpet; they've adorned numerous celebrities. He is known for mixing some street-wise aesthetics to his designs, which makes them appealing to young people.

Tom Ford

Tom Ford is a notable designer who has previously been creative fashion director at Gucci and Yves Saint Laurent. He is well known for his men's suit designs, and has notably designed for celebrities and politicians. Names like Michelle Obama, Justine Timberlake, and Beyonce are on his list. He brings a powerful sensual look to his style. He has designs ranging from men's wear, jewelry, and women's wear. He is also a well-regarded film director.

Christain Louboutin

Christain Louboutin is best known for his works with shoes. He says that entertainment was a strong inspiration for him, and one of his greatest fascinations was ladies dancing in high heels. Understanding them was understanding how women wanted their shoes to be. Whenever you see glossy red stiletto shoes, you know it may well be a Louboutin design.

Today the world is fast-paced, and while you can still make the best designs manually, there is also great pattern-making software available that makes the work very easy for you. With the use of such software, you can save time, energy, and resources. No need for the clutter that comes with cutting and gluing when you can do all that on a screen. You can easily store them in your device and make alterations and as many designs as you want for future use. They are quite flexible, and you do not have to be an expert to use them. The higher-range ones are a bit pricey, but they may be something to consider.

Here are some important and affordable pattern softwares that you should check out;

Computer-Aided Design Software: Softwares like Optitex, Gerber, Lectra are great for pattern makers and sewers. This software allows you to transform simple sketches to digital illustration, also making it easy to add measurements and grade patterns. It comes with a 2D and 3D effect.

Wild Things: This is another great software that helps you creatively draw and illustrate your designs, it also allows you to print them out, and it comes with a guide to give you step-by-step actions on how to use it. It also comes with a feature that helps you create embellishment and accessories for your design. And it's free!

Inkscape: This is a great professional drafting software. It allows you to draft patterns easily and can be used in 2D and 3D drawings. It is strictly for pattern drafting and works well in using shapes, objects, and freehand drawing to design your patterns.

GIMP: This is an excellent pattern making and sewing tool. It comes with a full package to draft and create designs and also to produce them. It allows you to integrate with other software tools and also offers features that help you to retouch and remake your designs quickly. It provides different file formats to save your documents and also comes with good tutorials.

More and more software tools will be created to help make fashion much easier, especially when it comes to design. Regardless, the fundamentals remain the same and will always be there to guide you to make good choices.

As the world continues to evolve, apparel designs have come and gone. There are some designs that have come and have remained constant while others become yesterday's trends. Historically, people would first think of body presentation and the need to conform to culture, social class, and moral standards. In today's world, creativity and comfort have become one of the major factors of design. We see it from long straight skirts to short skirts. There have been some great apparel designs over the years that have stood the test of time. These designs have remained relevant and continue to transcend passing fads.

The palazzo trousers: The palazzo trousers have been fashionable for a long time; they are quite comfortable and airy. They sit well on the female form and can be worn both formally and casually, depending on the design and fit. They normally hold the waist and drape down to the ankles and can be worn with pumps.

The Spanx: What would the ladies do without a pair of spanx? This apparel is a much-needed shapewear that has continued to be a favorite item in every woman's wardrobe.

Denim jeans: These are apparel designs that have been around for a long time. There is something about their comfort and fit that brings a casual balance to everything.

These designs continue to rock the world, and, most of the time, are redefined to be used again and again. From the straight skirt to a simple tee-shirt to a complicated ball gown by Alexander McQueen, fitting the form remains paramount. Hence, pattern fitting and alteration in fashion design is not a master to itself or apart from the individual. It is worthy of note that no matter how great a design might be, without a person to wear it, it is no more than useless. The goal remains fitting the form and highlighting its best assets while providing great comfort.

As a fashion student, this tells you that there is still much more to be done, and you are only a pencil and paper away from creating a new design that might amaze everyone. We can see that the world's best designers have one thing in common; they choose to push boundaries but also stick to the fundamentals. One area that was highlighted throughout this guide is the importance of understanding the fundamentals and basics. If you remember this, you will go far in your own journey of innovation.

www.ingramcontent.com/pod-product-compliance
Lightning Source LLC
Chambersburg PA
CBHW071448030726
47593CB00003B/946